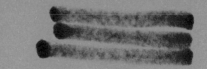

An Elephant in the Backyard

An Elephant in the Backyard

text and photographs by
RICHARD SOBOL

DUTTON CHILDREN'S BOOKS ❀ New York

For Daniel, who has learned the secrets of Wan Pen

Library of Congress Cataloging-in-Publication Data
Sobol, Richard.
 An elephant in the backyard / text and photographs by Richard Sobol.—1st ed.
   p. cm.
 Summary: Describes how special elephants are in the village of Tha Klang in Thailand
and looks at the life of one particular young elephant named Wan Pen.
 ISBN 0-525-47288-6
1. Asiatic elephant—Thailand—Tha Klang—Juvenile literature.
2. Elephants—Thailand—Tha Klang—Juvenile literature. [1. Asiatic elephant. 2. Elephants.
3. Endangered species. 4. Thailand.] I. Title.
SF401.E3S64 2004
636.9'676—dc22 2003052492

Published in the United States 2004
by Dutton Children's Books,
a division of Penguin Young Readers Group
345 Hudson Street, New York, New York 10014
www.penguin.com
Designed by Irene Vandervoort
Manufactured in China
First Edition
10 9 8 7 6 5 4 3 2 1

ACKNOWLEDGMENTS

I am grateful for the support and assistance of friends and colleagues, which allowed me to complete this book. For their hospitality, insights into elephant behavior, and the best home cooking, I am indebted to Prakit Klangpattana, Elephant Village headsman in Tha Klang, and his family, Somsri, Jak, and Muay. The Tourism Authority of Thailand aided in logistics and introduced me to my guides and translators, Komsan Suwannarat and Noppadon Tempsinpadung. Marion Darby, Rashana Pimolsindh, Jane Puranananda, and Concierge Adisorn of the Shangri-La Hotel gave me a home away from home in Bangkok. My friends in the Royal Thai Wildlife Protection and Anti-Deforestation Force who safeguard the elephants—Lieutenant Colonel Tevannuwat Aniruth Deva, General Salang Bunang, and Dr. Pasawat Srithai—encouraged me to undertake this project. Paul Seigel, Jak Severson, Russ Fill, Chris Wicke, and Cosmo endured torrential downpours, tropical sun, and frisky primates during my earlier visits to Thailand. Thanks to my agent and friend, Susie Cohen, and to my patient and insightful editors— Rosanne Lauer, Stephanie Owens Lurie, Susan Van Metre, Daniel Sobol, and Betty Bardige. Chalee Kioechui of the Baan Thai restaurant in Waltham, Massachusetts, who makes the best sticky rice and Pad Thai in North America, helped with the Thai language translations. Thanks to Irene Vandervoort for her lively design, which has brought this book to life.

And I am indeed grateful to Wan Pen for her grace, intelligence, and patience.

The Tourism Authority of Thailand can be reached online at www.tourismthailand.org for more information on travel to Thailand and to arrange overnight visits to Wan Pen and Tha Klang Elephant Village.

In most neighborhoods, elephants are way too big to keep in the backyard. When an elephant is sleepy, it needs a bed fifty times bigger than one used by a dog or a cat. When an elephant is thirsty, its drinking dish has to hold as much water as a full bathtub. To keep an elephant happy and fed, just one day's worth of food would fill an entire garage.

Today, there are only a few environments where elephants can live safely. Untamed elephants can live in the wild in open forests and fields far away from people and homes. Tame elephants usually live in zoos or in strong cages at circuses. In a small village in Thailand —Tha Klang—domesticated elephants roam freely, coming and going as they please.

Like most villages in Thailand, Tha Klang is filled with all kinds of people. Large families with mothers and fathers, grandparents, aunts, uncles, and children all live close together. The adults work as teachers, farmers, and silk weavers while the children study and play.

But what makes Tha Klang different from other villages is that it has elephants, too. For the children of Tha Klang, elephants are part of their families.

For thousands of years elephants have worked hard in Thailand. Wild elephants were caught in the deep forests and taught to respond to the commands of their trainers. They helped to transport people and cargo, worked on farms, and carried the king and his family to royal festivals. Tha Klang is famous in Thailand as the home of the strongest, smartest, and largest elephants in the country.

Jak, nine, and Muay, seven, are brother and sister. They have another sister, too, but she has four legs and weighs three thousand pounds. Her name is Wan Pen, and she is a four-year-old Asian elephant. She is friendly and gentle, happy to walk through the neighborhood with the children riding on her back, stopping to pick up friends who run alongside, eager for a ride. When Jak and Muay talk to Wan Pen, she raises her head, listening to them as they tell her in Thai: *Yood*, "Stop"; *Pai Dai*, "Go ahead"; *Leo Kwa*, "Turn right"; and *Leo Sai*, "Turn left."

Jak and Muay make driving an elephant look easy, almost as if they are simply parking a minivan in a tight space, edging gently left and right, forward and backward. Wan Pen turns carefully and gracefully, bending slightly as they guide her through the palm trees and gardens of Tha Klang. Although she seems to squeeze through these tight spaces easily, Wan Pen has already had two years of "driving school" with her own personal teacher— her *mahout*, Choy. Choy is a professional elephant trainer (*mahout* is the Thai word for *elephant trainer*) who will spend the next ten years working with just one elephant —Wan Pen. Once she is a teenager, Wan Pen will "graduate," and Choy will start training another baby elephant.

Even though there are eighty other elephants living in Tha Klang, Wan Pen is special. Her name made her famous. When elephants turn two years old, they have a birthday party to help them find a fitting name. Instead of cake, their families spread out all kinds of food for them to try. All elephants are vegetarians, but that doesn't mean they eat lightly. Large piles of fresh fruit, dozens of plants, and bright colorful flowers are all arranged as gifts for the baby elephant. Everyone watches closely to see what the elephant will eat first, since that will become its name. Lots of Thai elephants are named *Goui* and *Sappalot*—"banana" and "pineapple"—because these foods are sweet treats that they love to eat.

On Wan Pen's second birthday, she stood as the sun was setting and looked at all the treats placed in front of her but did not move toward any of them. At the moment she was just not hungry. Instead of grabbing for food, she raised her trunk up high, holding it straight into the air, and stretched it as if she were trying to touch the big, bright moon that shone overhead. And that became her name—Wan Pen, which means "full moon."

For Thai people, a full moon is a celebration. It is a time of feasting and prayer. Each month during the full moon they visit their temples to light candles and bring gifts. Wan Pen joins them in this monthly festival, and the people of her village believe that she brings them good luck.

While Jak and Muay attend school each day, Wan Pen goes to school, too. Choy is her full-time teacher. There are not any desks or blackboards in her classroom. She does not sit and learn the letters of the alphabet or how to count with numbers. Instead, her lessons look more like gymnastics class. Even though she weighs as much as a car and has a big fat belly, she learns to balance and walk on narrow boards and steps. She can bow and kneel, dance and shake her butt, and even raise her trunk to say hello or ask for food or drink. Her trunk has over forty thousand muscles in it, so Choy spends a lot of time teaching her all the ways that she can use it.

Wan Pen loves to play with the children after school, and her favorite game is soccer. All the kids want her to be on their team, but they never let her play goalie. No one would ever score if she sat down in the goal—all the balls would just bounce off her thick skin. The wide soft pads on the soles of her feet help Wan Pen to kick the soccer ball without exploding it. These spongy

cushions also help her walk on muddy ground in forests and swamps. Kicking with her round, flat feet and swinging her mighty trunk, she is the best shooter on the field, although sometimes she gets so excited that she kicks the ball into the wrong goal. Usually the final scores look more like a football or basketball game with high scores on both sides, but it doesn't matter— everybody enjoys the match.

Elephants have very rough, thick skin with stiff hairs that make it feel like splintery wood covered with little spikes. Bugs and insects like to crawl into the skin, which can be very uncomfortable for the elephant. This is one reason why they love to swim and take baths. The water and mud help to clean out the clusters of bugs that live in their deep folds and wrinkles. Wan Pen could sit under the hose and let Jak spray water over her all day. He has to force her to get up. Like most four-year-olds, she knows how to be lazy, too, and she is happy to sit back and enjoy this refreshing shower.

Wan Pen is one of the many elephants that live and train in Tha Klang. For thousands of years the elephants of Tha Klang and their cousins in smaller Thai training camps were taught to work deep in the forests, pulling out the heavy trees that were being cut for lumber. In Thailand and many other places, the trees were cut down faster than they were being replanted, and the forests disappeared. Both the loggers and the elephants lost their jobs. Today most elephants in Thailand help earn a living for their families by performing for tourists. Many visitors travel to Tha Klang to see how smart and athletic these wonderful elephants are.

When she is a few years older, Wan Pen will give visitors rides on her strong back, leading them on tours through the neighborhoods of Tha Klang. The money that Wan Pen earns will also help her family buy food and pay for school for Jak and Muay.

The village of Tha Klang sits snuggled between two rivers, the Chee and the Mun. Their muddy waters help to nurture the miles and miles of wet, green rice fields that grow all around. The rice helps to feed Jak and Muay and the other children and adults of the village. Beyond the rice fields are lush jungles with plenty of bamboo shoots and wild bananas that help satisfy the enormous appetites of all the elephants that live here. Wan Pen eats almost four hundred pounds of food a day. And she is still growing!

Tha Klang is a small knot of single-lane roads, only two of which are paved. Most of the roads are dirt and gravel mixed together with years and years of mashed elephant droppings. This may sound gross, but it's really just a lot of mixed-up vegetables and water that went through an elephant's stomach as if it were a huge food processor. When the hot, tropical sun bakes the droppings, they turn into a hard brown clay that makes a perfect coating for a country road—or an elephant-poop highway.

Tha Klang villagers live a traditional way of life, cooking in large pots over charcoal fires, growing vegetables and herbs in small gardens, raising silk-worms and spinning and weaving the precious threads, and training elephants much like their fathers and grand-fathers have done for hundreds of years. Elephants passing through the streets, backyards, or town squares are often unnoticed, except by the smallest children, who still point and giggle with delight. The elephants carefully step around toys, wicker chairs, rope hammocks, and cooking stoves. They move gracefully as they carry their floppy bulges of rough, brown skin through narrow paths and garden plots.

At night the village is very dark and quiet. Everybody goes to sleep early in order to rest and wake at sunrise to start work in the rice fields. Tha Klang's elephants need a lot of sleep, too. Some will lie down in the dusty yards and dirt patches ouside their families' homes, while others like Wan Pen will cross the river to sleep on a strip of soft grass.

Before Wan Pen sleeps, Choy will give her a jumbo bedtime snack of grass and soft fruits. With a fat, full belly, she will sleep soundly through the night, unless she wakes up to catch a peek at the moon.

Jak and Muay will have a snack, too; theirs will be something familiar like milk and cookies. And every night, they stroll with Wan Pen down the darkening trail to say good night before they crawl into their own beds. They are very lucky. Every night of the year, no matter how black the sky might be or how heavily the rain might be falling, they always get to say *"Ratri Sawad, Wan Pen"*: "Good night, Full Moon."

MORE ELEPHANT FACTS

- Elephants are the largest of all land animals.

- There are two basic elephant species—the African elephant and the Asian elephant (sometimes also called the Indian elephant). They can be recognized by their different shapes. The back of an African bends down in the middle; the Asian's back goes up in an arch. The Asian also has two bumps on its forehead. A good way to help identify them quickly is to look at the ears. The African elephants have larger ears that are shaped much like the continent of Africa. The Asian elephants have smaller ears that look like the shape of India.

- Asian elephants (like Wan Pen) are an endangered species. Approximately 25,000 Asian elephants live in the wild in Thailand, Sri Lanka, India, Indonesia, Vietnam, Laos, Nepal, Malaysia, Cambodia, Myanmar, and southern China. In Africa, the population is estimated to be 500,000. Twenty years ago, the worldwide population was thought to be as high as 1.4 million.

- Asian elephants can weigh up to 11,000 pounds and stand ten feet tall. African elephants can weigh up to 14,000 pounds and stand eleven feet tall.

- Many elephants have been killed illegally by poachers who try to sell their tusks. It is against the law to buy or sell elephant ivory in the United States, Canada, and one hundred other countries around the world.

- Elephants are vegetarians and eat up to 400 pounds of green leaves, bark, branches, fruit, and grass each day.

- Elephants have six sets of teeth. When one set wears down from chewing, the next set replaces it. When the last set wears down and the elephant can no longer eat, it will die of starvation.

- Tusks are incisor teeth that grow long. In Asian elephants they are usually found on the males only. Tusks help the elephants to dig in the ground for roots and to break apart thick tree bark.

- The average life span of an elephant is sixty years.

- The elephant's trunk is the longest nose of any animal and contains 40,000 muscles.

- Elephants can make a variety of sounds such as trumpets, growls, snorts, squeaks, rumbles, and roars. The sounds communicate information to other elephants.

- Elephants can run twenty-four miles per hour for short distances—twice as fast as any sprinter.

- The tail of an elephant has a few wiry hairs on the end that can be whipped around like a flyswatter to squash bugs that bite or burrow into the skin.